MW00977529

Seeds of a Nation

Maryland

Debbie Levy

KIDHAVEN PRESS™

THOMSON
GALE

San Diego • Detroit • New York • San Francisco • Cleveland
New Haven, Conn. • Waterville, Maine • London • Munich

© 2004 by KidHaven Press. KidHaven Press is an imprint of The Gale Group, Inc.,
a division of Thomson Learning, Inc.

KidHaven™ and Thomson Learning™ are trademarks used herein under license.

For more information, contact
KidHaven Press
27500 Drake Rd.
Farmington Hills, MI 48331-3535
Or you can visit our Internet site at http://www.gale.com

LIBRARY OF CONGRESS CATALOGING-IN-PUBLICATION DATA

Levy, Debbie.
  Maryland / by Debbie Levy.
    p. cm. — (Seeds of a nation)
Summary: Discusses the early history of Maryland beginning with the Native
Americans who have lived there for ten thousand years, through European
exploration and settlement, to statehood in 1788.
Includes bibliographical references and index.
  ISBN 0-7377-1447-6 (alk. paper)
  1. Maryland—History—Colonial period, ca. 1600–1775—Juvenile literature.
2. Maryland—History—Revolution 1775–1783—Juvenile literature. [1. Maryland—
History—Colonial period, ca. 1600–1775. 2. Maryland—History—Revolution,
1775–1783.] I. Title. II. Series.
  F184.L55 2004
  975.2'02—dc21

                                                        2003009406

Printed in the United States of America

Contents

Chapter One

Native Americans: Masters of Land and Water

Maryland is one of the smallest states in the United States. It ranks forty-second out of fifty in terms of territory. Yet, with more than 5 million people, Maryland ranks nineteenth in population in the United States, and sixth in population density. In addition, Maryland's Chesapeake Bay is the largest **estuary** in the entire nation. The Chesapeake was central to early life in Maryland and remains important today.

More than ten thousand years ago, the Chesapeake Bay did not yet exist. Instead, the Susquehanna River cut through the land. The river flowed north to south and emptied into the Atlantic Ocean. But things were changing on the continent of North America. The great glaciers were melting. Huge amounts of melted ice caused the Atlantic Ocean to rise. The Susquehanna River burst out of its banks. Ocean water flooded the Susquehanna's valley, and formed a giant estuary. This was the beginning of the Chesapeake Bay.

Rise of the Algonquian

By 1000 B.C., the Chesapeake Bay assumed the shape it has today. Native Americans built villages near the bay's shore and along the banks of its rivers. The Native Americans who settled in Maryland belonged to many tribes. On the western shore of the Chesapeake lived the Piscataway and Yaocomico tribes. The eastern shore was home to the Nanticoke, Pocomoke, Accohannock, and

Maryland's Place in the United States Today

Pennsylvania

West Virginia

Virginia

Delaware

Maryland

Wicomico. All of these tribes were part of a larger group called the Algonquian, named after the Algonquian languages that they shared.

Conflict between Native American tribes was a part of life, as they competed for hunting and fishing grounds. The Susquehannock, who moved to Maryland from Pennsylvania, made war against the Algonquian. But many Algonquian tribes in Maryland were peaceful and wanted only to tend their gardens, hunt for game, fish the waters, and raise their children.

Building a Village

The Algonquian built several types of homes. One of the most common was the wigwam. A wigwam was a small round hut built of young trees, called saplings, from which the bark was peeled. The Algonquian staked the saplings into the ground in a circle, then bent the tops together. They covered this dome-shaped frame with woven branches, animal skins, and bark.

A typical wigwam was ten to sixteen feet wide and housed one or more families. A small fire in a pit in the middle of the hut provided light, warmth, and protection against insects. Smoke escaped through an opening in the roof of the wigwam. The Algonquian usually cooked over large outdoor fires.

Algonquian villages were not large. For example, four to six families made up a typical village of the Pocomoke tribe on the Chesapeake Bay's eastern shore. A Piscataway village on the western shore might have twenty huts. Around their villages, the Algonquian built fences of tall wooden stakes to help keep out attackers.

The Algonquian build wigwams as homes, starting with a frame made from saplings.

Cycle of Seasons

Life for most of Maryland's Native Americans revolved around the types of foods that could be grown, gathered, or hunted during different seasons of the year. In spring and summer, villagers raised crops. In the fall, they harvested the food they had been growing. The people dried vegetables such as corn and beans, and stored them for use during the winter.

When the weather turned cold, Indian families often left their villages. They traveled to hunting territories, where they camped for months at a time. There they hunted animals such as deer, bear, rabbit, squirrel, partridge, and turkey. After a winter of hunting, the families returned to their villages to plant their gardens and start the cycle of seasons over again.

Living Off Land and Water

Native Americans divided their work between men and women. Men were in charge of hunting. They used traps to catch small animals, such as beavers, squirrels, and raccoons. To hunt larger game, such as white-tailed deer, the Indian men used different techniques. In one method,

A band of Native Americans hunts deer at night. Native Americans used the bow and arrow to hunt large animals.

they trapped groups of deer by lighting fires in a circle two or three miles wide. Slowly, the hunters moved the fires inward, creating a smaller circle. The frightened deer moved toward the center of the fire circle, until the hunters could kill them with bows and arrows.

Men were also in charge of fishing. The Chesapeake Bay was full of all kinds of seafood, including shellfish such as crabs, mussels, oysters, and clams, and many types of fish, including shad, perch, eel, and bass. Sometimes, Indian fishermen used spears or bows and arrows to kill fish. At other times, they fished with nets or used a weir, a fencelike trap made of twigs planted in the bottom of shallow streams.

Preparing Nature's Bounty

Women and children took care of growing crops in the gardens. They used tree branches and deer antlers to prepare the soil. Into the loosened earth, women planted seeds from corn, beans, squash, pumpkins, sunflowers, and tobacco. To keep birds from eating the seed, children sometimes acted as living scarecrows, sitting on platforms and making scary noises.

Native American women also prepared the deer and other animals that men killed during hunting expeditions. They skinned the animal and cut the meat from its carcass. They cooked some meat to be eaten right away and dried other meat to use later. When they finished preparing meat, women treated deerskins to make them suitable for clothing. For lightweight garments, they first scraped the fur from the hide. Then they softened the deerskin, sometimes using an oily paste made from deer brains, until it was smooth and comfortable. Women made these soft skins into short aprons, worn by both men and women. They also fashioned the deerskin into moccasins, leggings, and coats. To make clothing for cold weather, women left the fur on the hide.

Algonquian women were also responsible for cooking for their families. They stewed, grilled, and dried fish and meat. They served maize, or corn, often. Sometimes it was fresh off the cob. Other times, they mixed corn with other vegetables. The women also ground corn into meal and made corn pone, a type of bread, from cornmeal mixed with water. They baked the bread on flat stones heated in the fire.

Native Americans dry fish and meat over an open fire.

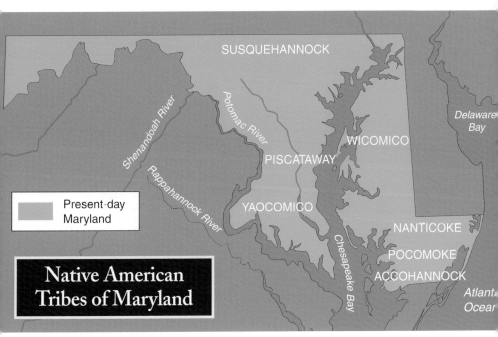

Native American Tribes of Maryland

SUSQUEHANNOCK

Shenandoah River

Potomac River

Rappahannock River

Delaware Bay

WICOMICO

PISCATAWAY

YAOCOMICO

Present-day Maryland

NANTICOKE

POCOMOKE

ACCOHANNOCK

Chesapeake Bay

Atlantic Ocean

Simple Comforts

By today's standards, life in Algonquian villages was primitive. Homes were cramped and smoky. Food was simple. But life was not bleak. Young people played sports such as lacrosse and games such as corncob darts. People enjoyed dancing and music, often as part of religious ceremonies.

Around ten thousand Native Americans lived in Maryland by the year 1600. Their lives were not exactly peaceful. But life among the Native Americans of Maryland followed certain patterns and offered some comforts. These patterns and comforts would not last for long. The Europeans were coming to America, and to Maryland.

Chapter Two

Chesapeake Explorers

E xplorers from Spain, France, Portugal, and England visited the North American east coast and Chesapeake Bay in the 1500s. They were hoping to find a northwest passage, a waterway through North America to Asia. They did not yet know that North America stretched three thousand miles from the Atlantic Ocean to the Pacific and that a shortcut to Asia did not exist. Explorers also hoped to find riches such as the gold and silver discovered in Central and South America.

In Maryland the explorers found neither a passageway to Asia nor precious metals. Despite this disappointment, European visitors were impressed by the region's beauty, climate, and wildlife. Giovanni da Verrazano was hired by the king of France to explore North America's Atlantic coast in 1524. In the first known description of the Maryland area by a European, he wrote, "We found wild roses, violets, and lilies, and many kinds of herbs and fragrant flowers different from ours."[1]

Chesapeake Explorers

More explorers sailed to the Chesapeake in the 1500s. Most came from Spain. The Spanish established some small settlements in the Chesapeake region, but they did not last.

English explorers also visited North America during this time. As early as 1498, John Cabot sailed along the

Giovanni da Verrazano explored the east coast of North America while looking for a route to Asia.

Atlantic coast. In the late 1500s, the English tried to create settlements in Newfoundland, Canada, and in North Carolina. But these efforts failed.

Yet people in England were still interested in establishing permanent settlements, or colonies, on America's east coast. Colonies in America could supply England with raw materials for its industries and goods for trading. Some leaders in England also thought that America was a good destination for the expanding class of poor people who needed a fresh start in life.

The English Arrive

In May 1607, three tiny English ships anchored in Virginia's James River after a voyage across the Atlantic Ocean. The men and boys on board set out to build a new colony near the river. They named their settlement Jamestown, after King James I.

The colonists struggled. They did not know how to grow food in the strange new land, and many starved. Others died of a disease called malaria. One of the colonists' leaders was Captain John Smith. He created rules for the settlers to follow. One rule required that people work if they wanted to eat the colony's food. Smith's strict rules helped the colony survive.

In the summer of 1608, Smith left Jamestown to explore the Chesapeake Bay. During this journey, he visited the area that later became Maryland. In his writings, Smith described the territory with awe. He was particularly amazed at the large number of fish in the bay. The fish were "lying so thicke with their heads above the

Captain John Smith made rules for the colonists in Jamestown to help them survive.

water," he wrote, that "we attempted to catch them with a frying pan."[2]

As Jamestown and other settlements in Virginia began to succeed, more people from England came to the

Maryland

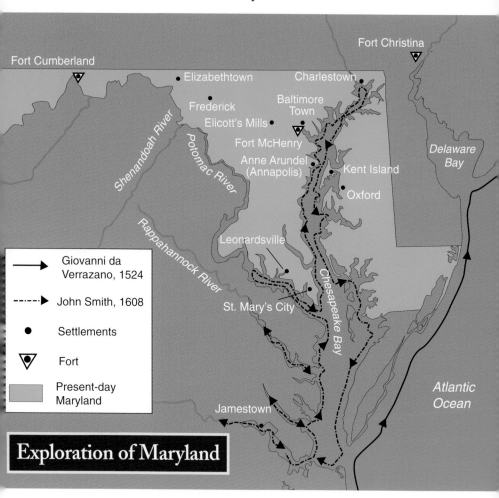

Exploration of Maryland

Legend:
- Giovanni da Verrazano, 1524
- John Smith, 1608
- Settlements
- Fort
- Present-day Maryland

New World. One such person was William Claiborne. Claiborne settled in Virginia but traveled throughout the Chesapeake Bay area and traded with Native Americans. In July 1631, he set up a trading post on an island in the bay north of Virginia. Claiborne named his post Kent Island. His settlers cleared land, planted farms, and traded with the Susquehannock and other Indians. Claiborne and the others considered their island an extension of Virginia. But this idea was about to be challenged by a new colony called Maryland.

The Calverts Are Coming

Like William Claiborne, George Calvert also looked to the New World for fortune and opportunity. He was a member of the court of King James I and had risen to the post of secretary of state of England. Calvert grew interested in colonization. In 1621, he bought land in Newfoundland, Canada. The king soon gave him more land in the area.

Calvert sent settlers to Canada to establish his colony in an area called Avalon. In a few years, one hundred men and women were living there. During this time, Calvert underwent an important personal transformation. In 1624, he became a Roman Catholic.

Colonists land at Jamestown, Virginia. The success of Jamestown encouraged more Europeans to come to the New World.

Maryland

Becoming a Catholic in England was very unpopular. The Church of England was the country's official religion, and it was headed by the king. People who were not members of the Church of England suffered discrimination. Roman Catholics, Quakers, and others were not permitted to practice their religion, and they were punished if they did. Catholics and others were not allowed to vote or hold public offices.

George Calvert wanted to establish a colony where Roman Catholics could practice their religion.

As a result of his conversion to Catholicism and other political disputes, Calvert had to resign his government positions. Still, King James I liked Calvert and in 1625 rewarded him for his past service by making Calvert a baron, or nobleman. Calvert received the title of Lord Baltimore and a large amount of land in Ireland. Calvert could pass down both his title and his lands to future generations.

In 1627 Lord Baltimore and his family and servants moved to Avalon. The people who had gone there earlier had built houses, a fort, a church, and other structures. Fish were plentiful, and the land held valuable copper. But life there was not perfect. The French also wanted to settle in that part of North America, and English settlers had to fight off French raiders. The weather was another problem. It was much colder than Lord Baltimore had expected. "From the middest of October to the middest of May," he wrote, "there is a sad face of winter upon all this land."[3]

A New Charter

After one harsh winter, Lord Baltimore decided to leave Avalon. He took his family south, to Jamestown. The climate there was warmer, but the welcome was not. Many Virginians objected to Catholics in their colony.

Even so, Lord Baltimore toured the Chesapeake Bay region and decided that he wanted to relocate his colony there. He sailed back to England to ask for land near Virginia. Naturally, Lord Baltimore was interested in the profits a colony would bring him. But he had another

Cecil Calvert accepts the charter to establish the colony of Maryland.

idea, too: He wanted to found a settlement where all Christians, particularly Roman Catholics, could live together and be free to practice their religions.

King James had died, but his son King Charles I was also friendly toward Lord Baltimore. The king granted Lord Baltimore 12 million acres north of Virginia and the Potomac River, on both sides of the Chesapeake Bay. Lord Baltimore died in April 1632 before the official documents for his colony were complete. His son, Cecil

Calvert, inherited his title and property, becoming the second Lord Baltimore. Cecil Calvert met with King Charles on June 20, 1632, to sign the charter creating the new colony. They named it Maryland, in honor of the king's wife, Queen Henrietta Maria.

The second Lord Baltimore had a charter. Now came the hard work: transforming a piece of land into a successful colony.

Chapter Three

Building a Colony

The second Lord Baltimore thought hard about the best way to build a colony. He knew that a successful colony needed people with knowledge of building and farming. To recruit skilled workers, Lord Baltimore offered every adult who came to Maryland one hundred acres of land. Bricklayers, carpenters, farmers, and blacksmiths all signed up to go to the new colony.

The new colony also needed people who were willing to work hard. Many of these people were very poor. The only way they could go to the New World was as **indentured servants**. In exchange for the cost of the ocean crossing, an indentured servant agreed to work for his employer for four to seven years. Lord Baltimore encouraged these laborers to come to Maryland by offering them land at the end of their indentured service.

Lord Baltimore made sure his settlers traveled with enough supplies. The settlers took plenty of food, drink, and tools, as well as seeds and roots to plant in Maryland. Good timing was also important. Lord Baltimore's colonists planned to leave England in autumn so they would arrive in Maryland the following spring. On this schedule, the new settlers could plant crops and harvest food before the next winter.

Voyage of the *Ark* and the *Dove*

In November 1633, two small wooden ships, the *Ark* and the *Dove,* sailed out of England and headed for the New World. On board were 150 to 300 people (no one knows for sure). Most were indentured servants, and most were

Rich farmland around the city of Baltimore was given to indentured servants who completed their time of service.

young men. Although Lord Baltimore intended to make his colony a haven for Catholics, fewer than twenty Catholics joined the expedition.

One important person was missing from the voyage: Lord Baltimore himself. The man behind Maryland feared that anti-Catholic Englishmen might persuade the king to take away his charter if he left England. So Lord Baltimore sent his younger brother, Leonard Calvert, to be governor of Maryland.

Almost as soon as the ships left England they ran into a terrible storm. In his journal of the voyage, one passenger, Father Andrew White, wrote, "So fierce a tempest [storm] broke forth . . . that it seemed every minute as if we must be swallowed up by the waves."[4] His ship, the *Ark,* lost sight of the *Dove.* The *Ark* rode out the storm and continued on its way.

The *Dove,* it turned out, was not lost. The two ships met again nearly two months later in the Caribbean Sea, on January 3, 1634. After resting and restocking supplies on Barbados Island, the settlers made their way north toward the Chesapeake Bay.

Finally, on March 25, 1634, passengers of the *Ark* and the *Dove* arrived in Maryland. They planted a large wooden cross on an island in the Potomac River. They named the island St. Clement's Island. Maryland was formally founded.

St. Mary's City

St. Clement's Island was too small for a settlement. So Governor Leonard Calvert and a group of men sailed up

The English traded goods with the Yaocomico Indians in exchange for land.

the Potomac River, where they found a village of Yao-comico Indians. The site had a deep harbor for ships and land that was already cleared. Governor Calvert went ashore to see whether the Native Americans would allow the English to settle there.

As it happened, the Yaocomico were planning to leave their village. They wanted to get away from the Susque-hannock, who regularly attacked them. The Yaocomico's unhappy situation was the settlers' good fortune. The tribe agreed to give the English their village in exchange for goods such as cloth, farming tools, and hatchets.

The newcomers unloaded their belongings and got to work building up the defenses of their village, which they named St. Mary's City. In keeping with Lord Baltimore's plan, the settlers planted food crops right away and never suffered for want of food. The Marylanders of St. Mary's harvested so much corn their first summer that they shipped the **surplus** to Boston to trade for salt fish and other goods.

The General Assembly

Under his charter from King Charles I, Lord Baltimore had the title of Lord Proprietor of Maryland. This gave him great powers. He could create towns, collect fees from colonists, and raise an army. He could also pass laws as long as he had the agreement of the free men of the colony. In 1635, the free men of Maryland gathered in St. Mary's City. The group was called the General Assembly. This assembly gave Maryland's colonists a voice in their own government.

An Argument with Virginia

Virginians opposed the creation of Maryland from the start. Lord Baltimore's charter interfered with their own land claims and trade in the Chesapeake. One Virginian felt especially threatened by the establishment of Maryland: William Claiborne.

Claiborne's fur trading business of Kent Island was thriving, and he wanted to keep it to himself. However, Kent Island was located within the new Maryland colony. Claiborne did not want to be under Maryland's rule and he argued that the king never intended to include in Maryland's territory areas that were already settled, such as Kent Island. The Calverts disagreed. They wanted the residents of Kent Island to follow Maryland law and pay fees to their colonial government, just like all other Maryland citizens.

This argument led to the first naval battle in the New World. It took place on April 23, 1635, in Pocomoke Sound, at the mouth of the Chesapeake Bay. This brief battle between Calverts' men and Claiborne's supporters did not resolve the argument, however. In 1638 the English government ruled that Kent Island belonged to Maryland. Despite this, Claiborne and his followers continued to resist Maryland's rule for years.

Two ships fire on each other in the Chesapeake Bay in the first naval battle of the New World.

Puritan Challenge

Back in England, different religious groups struggled for power. One group, the Puritans, took control of the government away from the Church of England for a time. The conflict reached Maryland, too. In February 1645, forces under the command of the Puritan ship captain Richard Ingle sailed to St. Mary's from England and took over the town and the colony. Governor Leonard Calvert and other Catholics fled to Virginia.

English Puritans took control of Maryland's government for a brief period of time.

The months that followed were known as "the troubles." Ingle and his followers destroyed the homes and property of colonists who did not want Maryland to be ruled by Puritans. Finally, in 1646, Governor Leonard Calvert organized a force of soldiers and recaptured St. Mary's.

The next year, Governor Calvert died. Soon after that, Lord Baltimore appointed a **Protestant**, or non-Catholic, governor. Most people in Maryland were Protestants, and Lord Baltimore wanted to show that Maryland remained a colony for all Christians, not only Catholics. Then in 1649, the Maryland Assembly passed the Toleration Act. This law said that all Christians, whether Protestant or Catholic, were entitled to practice their religion freely. Although the law protected only people who believed in Jesus Christ, it went further to protect religious freedom than any other law in the English-speaking world at that time.

Fate of Native Americans

As English colonists struggled over control of their colony, Maryland's Native Americans struggled with the loss of their homeland. On the Chesapeake Bay's western shore, many died of diseases like smallpox that the colonists brought to the New World. Others left Maryland. They moved north to Pennsylvania and New York to live with other tribes.

On the bay's eastern shore, Maryland officials forced many Native Americans off land that colonists wanted. The colony created **reservations** for some Native Americans, but these small tracts of land were no substitute for

Native Americans and English colonists clashed as the colonists expanded their settlements.

the vast hunting, farming, and fishing grounds the tribes had used for centuries. So, many eastern-shore Indians also moved north to live among other tribes. The land no longer belonged to America's native people. Maryland was firmly in the hands of the English colonists.

Chapter Four

The Way to Independence

Throughout the seventeenth century, Maryland continued to grow and change. In 1642, some four hundred settlers lived in the colony. By 1660, the population expanded to more than four thousand. Fifty years after that, more than forty thousand people lived in Maryland.

Most people living in Maryland were farmers. They grew several crops. One of the main crops was tobacco. The Maryland village of Georgetown, on the Potomac River, became a major port for shipping tobacco to England. On the Chesapeake Bay's eastern shore and in northern Maryland, planters raised wheat. And in western Maryland, settlers grew corn and flax, a plant used to make linen. The river town of Baltimore became a busy port for grain exports.

The Slave Economy

Maryland's tobacco farming led to the rise of slavery there. Planting, tending, and harvesting tobacco was hard work

Planners survey the site for the town of Baltimore. The town became a very busy port.

that required year-round labor. During most of the 1600s, farmers did the work with the help of white indentured servants. By 1700, though, few indentured servants were coming to Maryland. To keep profits high, tobacco planters needed a new source of unpaid laborers. They turned to African slaves.

The Maryland General Assembly passed laws to prevent slaves from gaining freedom. One law declared that black slaves and their children were to be slaves for life. (In the past, slaves who became Christians were freed.)

Other laws applied harsh punishments to slaves who tried to run away. These and other laws encouraged Maryland's colonists to hold slaves. Over the years, the number of slaves in Maryland grew, until they made up more than one-quarter of the colony's population.

Power Shifts

In 1675, Cecil Calvert, the second Lord Baltimore, died. His son Charles Calvert became the third Lord Baltimore and new Lord Proprietor of Maryland. Many colonists turned against the new Lord Baltimore, in part

African slaves arrive in Maryland. Colonists in Maryland used slaves to work their farms.

because he filled government jobs with Catholic relatives and friends. Maryland's General Assembly often refused to pass laws the new Lord Baltimore wanted.

In 1689, a group of Protestants, with the approval of authorities back in England, took over the colony's government from Lord Baltimore. The new government established the Church of England as the colony's official religion. Catholics lost the right to worship publicly or to hold government office. The government moved from St. Mary's, where people favored the Calverts, to a new capital farther north, a city called Annapolis.

The new Maryland government brought some positive changes. The government created public schools. It established regular postal service. During this time, members of the Maryland General Assembly also became experienced in debating and passing laws. And they began to stand up to the governor when they disagreed with his actions.

The Fourth Lord Baltimore

In 1715, Benedict Calvert became the fourth Lord Baltimore. He gave up Catholicism and joined the Church of England. Benedict Calvert asked King George I to restore Maryland to him and his family. The king agreed.

The Calverts were once again in charge of Maryland. But things were different. The members of the Maryland General Assembly were now used to challenging their government leaders when they disagreed with them. And by the mid-1700s, Marylanders had more and more reasons to disagree with their leaders.

The Stamp Act drew protests throughout the colonies.

Resisting English Taxes

In 1754, England and France began fighting a war for control of what is now Ohio and western Pennsylvania. The war lasted until 1763, but England finally won. France abandoned North America.

England was deeply in debt after the years of war. To raise money, the English government decided to impose a **tax** on its colonists. In 1765, England adopted the Stamp Act. Under this law, colonists had to print all newspapers, pamphlets, legal documents, and even playing cards on paper bearing special stamps sold by the

English. Money raised by this stamp tax went to the English government. Colonists were furious. They were willing to pay taxes to their own local governments in which they had a say. But they objected to paying taxes to a government across the ocean in which they had no voice or vote.

Throughout the colonies, riots broke out. In Maryland, angry mobs in Annapolis protested in the streets. Surprised by the colonists' reaction, England got rid of the Stamp Act by 1766.

Still, England was determined to collect taxes from its colonies. A few years later, the English government decided to tax tea. Most colonists did not like this tax any better. In December 1773, angry Massachusetts residents dumped a shipload of English tea in Boston Harbor, a protest known as the Boston Tea Party.

Rising Conflict

England reacted harshly to the Boston Tea Party. To punish the people of Boston, England ordered the city closed to shipping. England also required Bostonians to allow English soldiers to live in their homes.

Angry at these punishments, twelve of the thirteen colonies sent representatives to Philadelphia, Pennsylvania, in September 1774 to attend a meeting called the First Continental Congress. (Georgia did not send representatives.) The representatives discussed how to respond to England's actions. They decided to complain to the king and to stop all trade with England. Some representatives spoke of the need to become independent from England if things did not get better.

Anthony Stewart burns his own ship to destroy its cargo of English tea.

Marylanders also responded by conducting their own "tea party" in October 1774. The *Peggy Stewart*, a ship owned by Maryland merchant Anthony Stewart, sailed into Annapolis Harbor loaded with tea from England. Annapolis residents were furious. Stewart apologized publicly for importing the tea. Then he ran the ship aground in the harbor and set it on fire.

Moving Toward Independence

In the spring of 1775, a battle broke out between colonists and English soldiers in Massachusetts. Marylanders supported the Massachusetts colonists. However, they did not support a final break from England. Many Marylanders felt that they had as much independence as they needed. They did not see the need for a war or formal independence.

Much as Marylanders hoped for peace, events were moving in a different direction. In June 1776, Virginia asked the Continental Congress to declare independence. At first, Maryland still hesitated. Finally, though, Maryland's representatives joined with the other colonies and voted to declare—and fight for—independence from England.

Benjamin Franklin makes a plea for independence from England. Maryland voted in favor of independence.

The American Revolution had begun. Maryland's soldiers fought in the colonists' army. The Chesapeake Bay swarmed with ships and troops from both sides. Maryland carpenters built warships, and Maryland farmers supplied soldiers with wheat.

New State, New Nation

Even as the war was being fought, Marylanders began to create a new government in their newly formed state. In 1776, they wrote a constitution that did away with the official church and guaranteed religious freedom for all Christians. Catholics could now hold office, vote, and worship publicly for the first time since 1689. The constitution also created a two-house legislature, with a house of **delegates** and a senate. Under the new constitution, the legislature chose the governor.

In October 1781, the Americans defeated the English. Two years later, England and the new United States of America signed a peace treaty. The thirteen colonies had become a single, independent nation.

A New Capital

The new nation did not have a permanent capital at first. New York City served as the temporary capital beginning in 1788. But George Washington, the country's first president, favored a site on the Potomac River. In 1790, Congress voted to build the nation's capital on a square of land along the Potomac River. Maryland donated its side of the square and Virginia donated land across the river. This federal district, one hundred square miles in area,

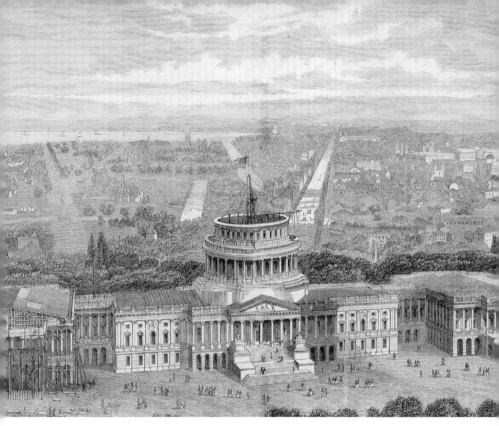

Washington, D.C., was built on land that used to be part of Maryland.

was named the District of Columbia, after Christopher Columbus. The capital city was called Washington. Later, the capital became known as Washington, D.C.

Under pressure from Virginia businessmen, the U.S. Congress gave that state back its part of the federal district in 1846. Ever since then, the nation's capital has stood on a site that was once part of Maryland.

Maryland was founded on a promise of religious liberty. It did not always keep that promise, but it did come back to it by the time of statehood. Like Maryland's Chesapeake Bay, which took shape slowly but surely over many years, the state of Maryland moved slowly but surely toward independence and liberty.

Facts About Maryland

Population: 5,296,486 (in 2000)

Land area: 12,407 square miles (land and water); 9,774 square miles of land

State capital: Annapolis

Nicknames: Old Line State and Free State

State song: "Maryland, My Maryland"

State bird: Baltimore oriole

State dog: Chesapeake Bay retriever

State fish: striped bass (also called rockfish)

State crustacean: Maryland blue crab

State insect: Baltimore checkerspot butterfly

State boat: skipjack

State sport: jousting

State flower: black-eyed Susan

State tree: white oak

Economy: services (technical, medical, lodging), trade (wholesale and retail sales), printing, federal government jobs, construction, manufacturing (electronic equipment, scientific instruments, paints, chemicals), food processing (soft drinks, spices, seafood, poultry), agriculture, and seafood

Famous people: Benjamin Banneker (astronomer, mathematician, surveyor of Washington, D.C.), Clara Barton (founder of the American Red Cross), John Wilkes Booth (assassin of President Abraham Lincoln),

Maryland

Samuel Chase (Supreme Court justice), Billie Holiday (singer), William Julius "Judy" Johnson (baseball player), Francis Scott Key (lawyer and author of the "Star Spangled Banner"), Thurgood Marshall (Supreme Court justice), Edgar Allan Poe (writer), Cal Ripkin Jr. (baseball player), Babe Ruth (baseball player), Roger Taney (Supreme Court chief justice), Harriet Tubman (abolitionist)

Notes

Chapter 2: Chesapeake Explorers

1. Quoted in Worcester County, Maryland History, http://skipjack.net.
2. Quoted in Donald Marquand Dozer, *Portrait of the Free State: A History of Maryland.* Cambridge, MD: Tidewater, 1976, p. 23.
3. Quoted in Sandy Shoemaker, *Where Maryland Began . . . the Colonial History of St. Mary's County.* Leonardtown, MD: Heritage, 2000, p. 13. www.somd.lib.md.us.

Chapter 3: Building a Colony

4. Father Andrew White, "Narrative of a Voyage to Maryland, 1633–34," The Society of the Ark and the Dove Home Page. www.thearkandthedove.com.

Glossary

delegate: Person that represents others.

estuary: Body of water in which saltwater from the ocean mixes with freshwater from a river.

indentured servant: Person who is bound by contract to serve another for a period of time.

Protestant: A Christian who is not a member of the Catholic Church.

reservation: Territory that is set aside for Native Americans to use.

surplus: Extra amount beyond the amount that is needed.

tax: A fee paid to a government authority.

For Further Exploration

Books

Michael Burgan, *America the Beautiful: Maryland.* Danbury, CT: Grolier, 1999. This book describes the geography, plants, animals, history, economy, culture, and people of Maryland.

Dennis Brindell Fradin, *From Sea to Shining Sea: Maryland.* Chicago: Childrens Press, 1994. This book gives an overview of Maryland's history, geography, and people.

Vera F. Rollo, *The Black Experience in Maryland.* Lanham: Maryland Historical Press, 1984. The history of African Americans in Maryland, from the first settlers to modern times, is highlighted in this engaging book.

————, *Your Maryland: A History.* Lanham: Maryland Historical Press, 1993. This book relates the story of the state's history, from the earliest Native American inhabitants to modern Maryland.

Sandy Shoemaker, *Where Maryland Began . . . the Colonial History of St. Mary's County.* Leonardtown, MD: Heritage, 2000. Also at: www.somd.lib.md.us. An account of early times in Maryland, this book provides detailed information about what life was like in a Native American village, the settlers' voyage to America, St. Mary's, farming, and slavery.

Websites

MD Kids' Page Home Page (www.mdkidspage.org). A picture-rich website, produced by the Maryland Office of the Secretary of State, offers information about Maryland, ranging from history and geography to famous women and places to visit.

Maryland Welcome Kids Room (www.mdisfun.org). Created by the Maryland Office of Tourism Development, this website has a special section for young people, with information about history and geography as well as Maryland-based word puzzles.

Index

Maryland